Project Management
The
CommonSense Approach

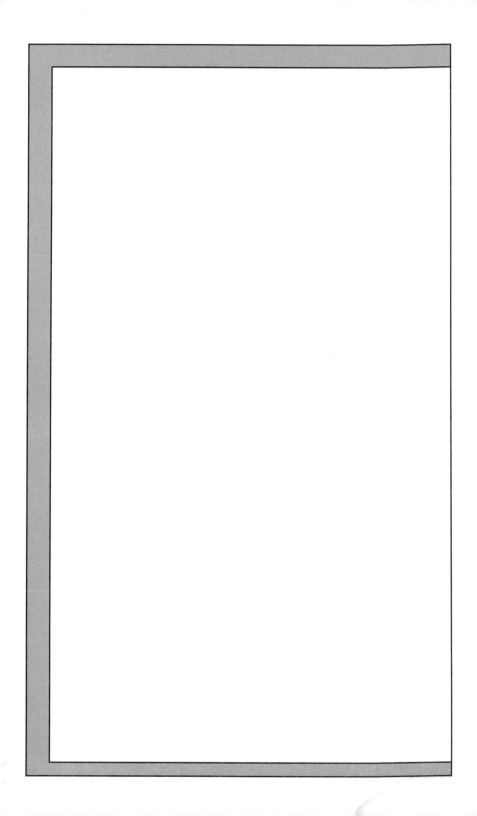

Project Management
The
CommonSense Approach

By
Lee R. Lambert, PMP
Erin Lambert, MBA

LCG PUBLISHING

COLUMBUS, OHIO

Illustrations By: Dick Bartlett

Library of Congress Catalog Number 00-191014

LCG Publishers, (614) 792-6582, or email
books@lambertconsultinggroup.com
www.LambertConsultingGroup.com

About the Authors

Lee R. Lambert, PMP

Chief Executive Officer
Lambert Consulting Group, Inc.
Phone: 614-792-6582
Fax: 614-792-6583
E-mail: lee@LambertConsultingGroup.com

Lee R. Lambert, PMP, founder and CEO of Lambert Consulting Group, Inc., is an honored and distinguished member of the project management community. Having started his career in project management in 1968 with General Electric, Lee spent 15 years in the trenches working hands-on with project management techniques and tools. During a distinguished corporate career, he held several senior project management positions with major U.S. corporations, including General Electric, Lawrence Livermore Laboratory and Battelle Memorial Institute. Among his extensive client list are IBM, Prudential Insurance, Monsanto, Sprint, Motorola, AT&T, CitiGroup, Nationwide Insurance, American Electric Power, Global Commerce Services, SAP Labs, Bechtel and National City Mortgage. To-date Mr. Lambert has trained over 25,000 students, in 21 countries, on the value-added use of the project management process and its associated tools and techniques. In 1981, he was a founding member of the five person team that formulated and implemented the Project Management Institute's (PMI) Project Management Professional (PMP1) Certification Program, now recognized as the world's standard in the profession of project management.

Mr. Lambert's consulting efforts have included four successful Enterprise-wide project management process development and implementation assignments. He has long been considered one of the world's leading project management educators. His humorous, creative, and effective common-sense-based learning facilitation style has been emphatically praised by thousands of students throughout the world.

In addition to serving as the lead trainer for Lambert Consulting Group, Inc., Mr. Lambert serves on the American Management Association's (AMA) Project Management Curriculum Development Council and is one of the senior instructors for George Washington University's Masters Certificate in Project Management curriculum. As an author, Mr. Lambert's publications include 26 journal articles and two books, including the most widely distributed text on the Earned Value Management System (EVMS) in the project management field, <u>The CommonSense Approach to Project Management: *Using Earned Value to Balance the Triple Constraint*</u>. He serves on the Editorial Review Board for *PMNetwork* and the *Project Management Journal*, has contributed two chapters to the AMA's critically acclaimed *Project Management Handbook* and has recently been cited in the Josey-Bass publication, <u>Creating the Project Office</u>, for his pioneering efforts in successfully developing corporate project offices. Mr. Lambert was the Master of Ceremonies for the ProjectWorld 2000 Conference in Boston and currently instructs workshops and makes technical presentations regularly at the PMI Symposia, ProjectWorld Conference, and the American Association of Cost Engineers International Symposia.

In 1995, Mr. Lambert was given the coveted Distinguished Contribution Award by PMI for his sustained dedication and contribution to the growth of the project management profession.

ERIN LAMBERT, MBA

Chief Operating Officer
Lambert Consulting Group, Inc.
Phone: 614-792-6582
Fax: 614-792-6583
E-mail: erin@LambertConsultingGroup.com

Erin Lambert, MBA, has been providing business consulting services for Lambert Consulting Group, Inc. since 1993, serving clients such as AirTouch Cellular (now Verizon Wireless), ECNext, Nextel Communications, National City Mortgage, Bechtel Nevada and ICG Communications. She has worked extensively in the international arena and in 1992, presented the results of her work in the area of Cause and Effect Relationships at an International Symposium in the Middle East. In recognition of her stellar efforts, she was awarded a position at Harvard University's John F. Kennedy School of Government, where she was responsible for researching and writing proposals for multi-million dollar development projects. While at Harvard, her responsibilities also included organizing and managing the JFK School of Government's international lecture series, featuring well-known dignitaries such as, Yasser Arafat and Itzak Rabine.

In 1999, Miss Lambert received her MBA from the Fisher College of Business, at The Ohio State University, with a double major in Marketing and Operations Management and a minor in Consulting. While there, she served as the Vice President of the MBA Association and was awarded a scholarship for her paper on Mass Customization and Its Role in Today's High Technology Environment.

Table of Contents

Figures

A STRATEGIC DEFINITION OF PROJECTS

"Projects are the means society and organizations use to create, to change and to build. Because of the importance of projects, society and organizations must understand the process and learn to manage projects successfully, or they will be forced aside by those who do."

Durrill and Ellsworth
Modern Project Management

Projects Make the World Go Around

1

WHAT IS PROJECT MANAGEMENT?

According to the Project Management Institute's PMBOK*, Project Management is the application of knowledge, skills, tools, and techniques to project activities in order to meet or exceed stakeholder needs and expectations from a project. Meeting or exceeding stakeholder needs and expectations invariably involves balancing competing demands among:

- Scope, time, cost, and quality.
- Stakeholders with differing needs and expectations.
- Identified requirements (needs) and unidentified requirements (expectations).

The term project management is sometimes used to describe an organizational approach to the management of ongoing operations. This approach, more properly called management by projects, treats many aspects of ongoing operations as projects in order to apply project management to them.

A TACTICAL VIEW OF A PROJECT

Organizations identify work. Work generally involves either operations or projects, although the two may overlap. Operations and projects share many characteristics; for example, they both are:

- Performed by people.
- Constrained by limited resources.
- Planned, executed, and controlled.

Operations and projects differ primarily in that operations are ongoing and repetitive, while projects are temporary and unique. A project can thus be defined in terms of its distinctive characteristics—a project is a temporary endeavor undertaken to create a unique product or service. Temporary means that every project has a definite beginning and a definite end. Unique means that the product or service is different in some distinguishing way from any similar products or services.

Projects are undertaken at all levels of the organization. They may involve a single person or hundreds of people. They may require less than 100 hours to complete. Some take thousands. Projects may involve a single unit of one organization, engage multiple organizational units (cross-functional), or may span organizational boundaries as in joint ventures, alliances and partnerings. Projects are often critical components of the performing organizations' business strategy. Projects are the fabric of our organizational society. Projects come from anywhere and everywhere.

They touch every part of an organization. Examples of projects include:

- Developing a new product or service.
- Effecting a change in structure, staffing, compensation or culture of an organization.
- Designing a new transportation capability.
- Developing or acquiring a new or modified information system.
- Constructing a building or facility.
- Running a campaign for political office.
- Implementing a new or improved business procedure or process.
- Relocating personnel or equipment (logistics).

The fact is; if you have any project, you and the project will benefit from the use of the Earned Value Management System concepts.

INTRODUCTION

Using the Earned Value Management System (EVMS), as described by the Department of Defense Regulation DoD 5000.2-R and similar requirements from the Federal Aviation Administration (FAA), National Aeronautic and Space Administration (NASA) and other government agencies, is not an option for many organizations performing work on highly visible, government funded projects.

Usually, EVMS (aka; Cost/Schedule Control System Criteria or C/SCSC) compliance is mandatory as one of the terms and conditions of large, complex government contracts.

However, when it comes to application of the Basic Earned Value techniques; the fact is that the size or type of the project doesn't really matter all that much.

The benefits of Earned Value concepts are real and can be realized on any project—large or small—providing sincerity, honesty, and **common sense** are at the heart of the application—even on projects where the use of EVMS is not mandated.

COMMON SENSE

If the formerly recognized C/SCSC stood for "Common Sense Cost & Schedule Comparison" then users should now consider that EVMS means "Every Variance Means Something." The user's job is to determine what that "something" is and then decide what (if anything) to do about it. Project Management practitioners must never forget, no matter how sophisticated or "fast" the data delivery process, it will not provide "answers" – but it will more clearly identify the "questions." Project Management professionals must define the questions and seek the truth as they provide the answers.

It should be noted that not everyone agrees that Earned Value is the best project management approach.

But, recent investigations have revealed that many of these same critics are subtly and carefully picking and choosing various components of the Earned Value process for use on their projects—and finding them to be extremely valuable and productive tools.

Since the DOD dropped the bomb onto the Project Management scene in the 60's, Earned Value has become a proven process that provides exceptional benefits for project planning, monitoring and decision making.

It delivers what has been difficult to attain in the most commonly used approaches to project management: distinct, automatic integration of the project's triple constraint—scope, time and cost.

Thus, conscientious use of the Earned Value concepts will create a realistic and objective performance measurement baseline (PMB) for most projects. This performance measurement baseline becomes the project management centerpiece in work scope definition, accomplishment statusing, problem or opportunity (real or perceived) identification, trending/forecasting, corrective action definition and, when needed, project replanning.

Today's managers constantly strive to discover methods or techniques that will enable them to fill the void that often exists in the availability of specific, timely and accurate project information to support their vital project and/or business decisions. Earned Value is one of those methods! We want to be completely candid about our opinion of the Earned Value method; we think, as an information producing process it is the ultimate! But our philosophy as longtime users of many project management systems/processes must be clear—if the maximum benefit is to be realized:

"Ask not what you can do for the PM process, ask what the PM process can do for you!"

The PM users must constantly be wary of the level of sophistication available to them in today's "at your finger tips" state of automation. Unfortunately, we may have created the proverbial "monster." Too many times the result of all this progress in both the volume and speed of data processing and distribution leads to an organization being able to; "Deliver bad project information–faster!" Following the logic, this phenomena then, of course, leads to; "Bad decisions being made–faster!"

ADVANTAGES

Project Planning will improve dramatically as work content at the actual performance level is defined and timed (not high level summary, passage of time or the availability of resources), thus becoming the focus for defining realistic project implementation expectations. In other words, what will you get when your money is gone?

Schedule Variances will be objectively isolated and quantified in terms of the actual work accomplished compared with work planned to be accomplished (not budget planned versus actual cost incurred or the mere passage of time as used in more traditional project tracking approaches).

Cost Variances will be true cost variances and will be measured in terms of the cost associated with the actual work output compared to planned cost for the same work output. Cost variances are not distorted by linear (passage of time based) schedule performance and, therefore, reflect a true cost-to-produce variance for a specific work output, regardless of the time of the output.

Performance Trends are linked directly to timely accomplishment of work and the cost of that same work and provide clear vision to what can be expected in the future. This information facilitates critical decision making, while there is still adequate time to implement cost effective, time efficient corrective actions.

Communication Effectiveness (based on the dramatically improved timeliness, accuracy, and clarity of the project information used to initiate the communication process) will improve substantially as the degree of subjective assessment of work progress and associated potential misinterpretation at all levels of the project and the organization are drastically reduced.

Training and Professional Development is facilitated by consistent application of the fundamental Earned Value concepts on all types of projects. Professional project management training and development should have, at its heart, established, effective and realistic methods of defining mutually agreeable expectations and measuring individual, team and organizational performance against those performance standards. The Earned Value concept provides these proven methods. Whether a company or project utilizes a formal project management system (detailed policies and procedures and tools) is not as critical as one might think. However, providing consistent PM methodology is paramount. With it…Earned Value will work!

COMMON SENSE

Never forget that if Earned Value is to add value, it MUST be an integral part of a comprehensive project requirements definition, planning and data gathering process. It would be ludicrous to think that merely adopting Earned Value techniques will enhance one's ability to effectively track and manage projects. Remember, there's no free lunch!

CHALLENGES

Planning time required during the early stages of the project, to create a meaningful performance measurement baseline, increases significantly using Earned Value. This "front end" investment of time flies in the face of the more traditional management philosophies pertaining to project planning: "We don't have time to do it right, but we do have time to do it over, and over, and over, and…" or, "We don't have time for planning, we've got work to do!"

Objective methods of planning and statusing work must be determined, established and used. Subjective assessment or determination of work accomplishment, i.e. percent complete, simple passage of time, expenditure of money, spend rate, mere quantity–count of milestones, etc., will lead to information distortion and potentially ineffective use of the Earned Value concept. In fact, if objective measures of work progress cannot be established, the Earned Value approach will add little, if any, value to the project management decision making process.

Integration of the Earned Value concepts with the organization's financial accounting system becomes crucial. Since Actual Cost (AC/ACWP) is one of the three key Earned Value based data points, linkage of timely, accurate financial accounting information to its associated project work content framework (Work Breakdown Structure) is very important.

Note: Lack of this accounting integration is not "fatal" to the use of Earned Value, but alternate approaches, i.e. Accrual Accounting require additional effort to maintain a "pure" Data–to–Work relationship.

Discipline (Human Support System) in the use of the Earned Value concepts will be required to maintain the work content based reality of the project performance measurement baseline and to assure that the integrity of the information that results from the ongoing use of Earned Value is maintained. Changes to the PMB must be closely monitored, thoroughly evaluated, and appropriately approved.

SUMMARY

Earned Value isn't magic, it isn't the cure–all for project problems. Earned Value is nothing more than another of the many project management tools (albeit, one of the best) available.

DO YOU BELIEVE IN MAGIC?

Informed and supportive users will enable Earned Value to become one of the most meaningful, effective and efficient tools a project management professional has available in the ever expanding PM "tool box." Like any other tool, the more Earned Value is used the more confident the users become and the more meaningful contribution the tool will make to the ultimate end product: A successful project!

But remember:

CHAPTER 1

HOW EARNED VALUE WORKS FOR THE ORGANIZATION

The material that follows will expose you to some of the key characteristics that make the Earned Value approach one of the most powerful and productive concepts utilized in managing today's challenging projects in private, commercial or government environments.

In the world of Earned Value, the role of the Control Account Manager (CAM) is the pivotal position in the process. The Project Manager and all of the other traditional project management contributors are active participants in Earned Value and certainly have significant responsibilities that can't be underestimated. However, because of the critical role and the strategic positioning in the project data/information (Figure 1) flow process of the CAM, it is this role that will ultimately determine the effectiveness of Earned Value.

This material is targeted at helping the CAM in planning and managing the assigned Work

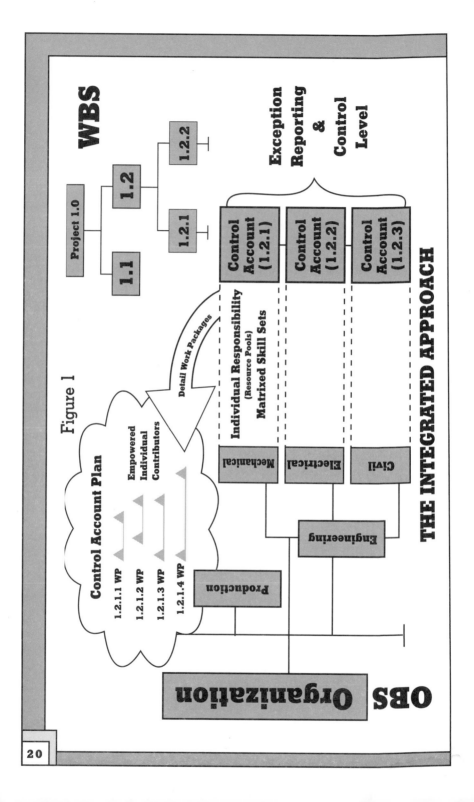

Figure 1

THE INTEGRATED APPROACH

Packages. The information is presented in easy to follow form. The Earned Value process is essentially the same at all levels of the project organization, in its application, only the level of detail or "information summary" changes.

Individual components of the formal Earned Value application address Work Authorization (including planning) through Project Reporting and Corrective Action Implementation. Descriptions of Control Accounts, Authorized Work Packages and Planned Work Packages have been emphasized due to their significance in the Earned Value approach in general, and specifically, their potential for enhancing the ability of the user to successfully meet the project requirements. Maintaining strategic and tactical consistency (at least from a management information perspective) throughout the life of the project is promoted by this integrated approach to planning and executing project work (Figure 2).

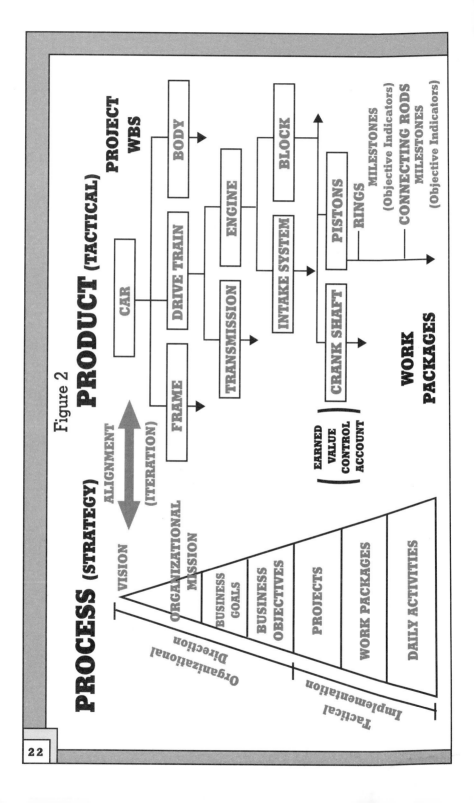

Figure 2

UNDERSTANDING EARNED VALUE'S FUNDAMENTAL STRUCTURE

Earned Value can only be successful if the users understand the concepts and recognize the need for a vertical hierarchical relationship between all the units of work to be performed on a project.

NOBODY KNOWS WHAT IT IS!
... IT JUST SITS THERE

This hierarchical relationship is established via the Work Breakdown Structure (WBS). Work is performed at the lowest levels of the WBS (Work Packages), therefore, these critical work subdivision elements have particular significance when it comes to achieving the most beneficial results from using Earned Value (Figure 2).

CONTROL ACCOUNT

The Control Account (CA) is the focus for Defining, Planning, Monitoring, and Controlling because it represents the work associated with a single organizational unit. Earned Value "comes together" at the CA level, which includes work scope, budgets, schedules, responsibility assignments, cost collection, progress assessment, problem identification and corrective actions. Detail Work Package plans typically exist one level below the Control Account. These Work Packages comprise the integrated logic network (precedence diagram). And, based on dependent input–output relationships, define the critical path.

Day–to–day work management is accomplished at the Work Package level. Most management actions taken at the CA level are on an "exception" basis in reaction to significant problems identified when WP information is summarized at the CA (See Figure 9).

The level selected for establishment of a CA must be carefully considered to ensure that work will be properly defined in discrete, manageable units (Work Packages) with work content well defined and responsibilities clearly delineated, and assigned.

AUTHORIZED WORK PACKAGE

An Authorized (sometimes called "open") Work Package (AWP) is a detailed effort that is identified by the Control Account Manager (CAM) for accomplishing work within a CA. An AWP has these characteristics:

• The AWP represents units of work at the levels where the work is performed (Work Package).

• An AWP is clearly distinct from all other Work Packages, and is usually performed by a single organizational element.

• An AWP has a scope of work, scheduled start and completion dates (with interim milestones, if applicable), which are representative of physical accomplishment.

• An AWP has a budget or assigned value expressed in terms of dollars (labor/material) and/or labor hours.

- Duration of an AWP is relatively short (PMBOK suggests ~80 hours of effort) unless the AWP is subdivided by discrete value milestones (objective indicators) that permit objective measurement of work performed over time.

- The AWP schedule is carefully integrated with all other project schedules.

PLANNING WORK PACKAGE

If an entire CA cannot be subdivided into detailed AWPs, far-term effort is identified in larger Planned Work Packages (PWPs) for far–term budgeting and scheduling purposes. This planning approach (sometimes called Horizon or Rolling Wave Planning) significantly reduces the impact of changes on far–term work that is frequently planned in too much detail, too soon.

The budget for a PWP is identified specifically according to the work for which it is intended. It may be generally time–phased, and have controls, which prevent its budget's use in performance of other work. The PWP budget is included in the PMB. Eventually, all work in Planned Work Packages will be planned to the appropriate level of detail and converted to Authorized Work Packages.

UNDERSTANDING EARNED VALUE'S THREE MOST VITAL DATA ELEMENTS

PLANNED VALUE WORK SCHEDULED—PV/BCWS

Planned Value is simply the amount of resources (human and other), usually stated in dollars, that are expected to be consumed to accomplish a specific scope of work. The PV is more commonly known as the spend plan, or cost estimate, and has been employed in the world of project management since its beginning. In Earned Value applications, the emphasis is placed on achieving a direct correlation between the scope of work to be completed (work content) and the amount of resources actually needed to accomplish the work.

ACTUAL COST OF WORK PERFORMED—AC/ACWP

In Earned Value AC is simply the amount of resources, usually stated in dollars, that were actually expended in accomplishing a specific scope of planned work, during a specific time period. The AC is more commonly known as the actual incurred cost, or actuals, and has also been employed in the world of project management since its beginning. These actuals are obtained via organizational reporting systems or through an accrual process.

VALUE OF WORK PERFORMED—EV/BCWP OR "EARNED VALUE" (See Figure 3)

EV is Earned Value's measure of the amount of work actually accomplished, stated in terms of the budget assigned to accomplish that specific scope of work. The work accomplishment status, as determined by those responsible for completion of the work, is converted to a data element and becomes the focal point of all status and analysis activities that follow. EV is the only new data element required when utilizing Earned Value management techniques. EV, when compared with PV and AC, provides the foundation for comprehensive, realistic management evaluations, projections and (if necessary) corrective actions regarding cost and schedule conditions.

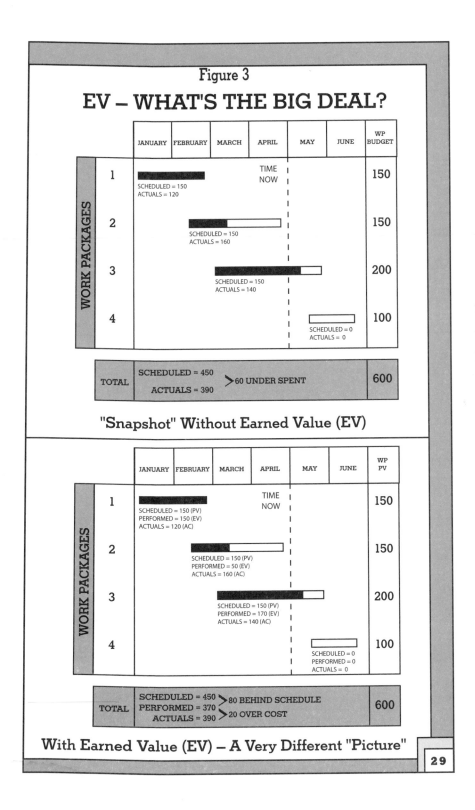

Figure 3
EV – WHAT'S THE BIG DEAL?

"Snapshot" Without Earned Value (EV)

With Earned Value (EV) – A Very Different "Picture"

29

CHAPTER 2

WORK AUTHORIZATION

All project work, regardless of origin, shall be described and authorized through the Work Authorization (WA) process, an integral part of Earned Value. Earned Value relates not only to work authorization, but also planning, scheduling, budgeting, and elements of project control, all of which reflect the definition and flow of work through the functional organizations.

Although the CAM is most concerned with the Work Authorization process at the Authorized Work Package (AWP) and control account (CA) levels, the total process is presented here to provide the CAM a sense of his/her role in the total work process. The work flow is traced from customer authorization through project change authorization:

1. Initial Authorization

   • Contract/Project "go ahead"
   • Project Scope Changes

2. Work Authorization

  • The organization provides authorization to the Project Manager (PM) to start work via some form of Project Directive (PD). The PD approves total project scope of work and funding levels.

3. WBS Planning Target Authorization

  • WBS Managers prepare WBS Planning Target Authorization
  • Project Manager approves WBS "target budget" goal for expansion to CA level

• WBS "target" is later replaced by the WBS budget rollup of all CA's

4. Control Account Planning Target Authorization

  • CAM prepares CA "target budget" goal for expansion to Work Packages
  • CA "target" is later replaced by CA budget rollup of all planned WP's

5. Change Control (in conjunction with an organization's existing configuration management procedures)

  • The CAM submits, or signs, a "marked–up" Work Package to show any internal replanning or any customer contractual baseline change that:

    1) alters work scope or approach by addition/deletion causing CA budget adjustments
    2) causes adjustment of scope or budget between CA's

  • Work Package Change Record (WPCR) is completed for audit trail of baseline revisions (baseline maintenance)

• The PM or delegated representative authorizes the add/delete transactions to Management Reserve if the budget adjustment is outside the single Cost Account

Note: Parties to the original budget agreements must approve revisions.

• The CA budget cannot be changed by such actions as:

> 1) cost overruns, or cost underruns due to performance
> 2) changes that affect project/ program schedules or milestones because of work acceleration or work slippage
> 3) retroactive adjustments

PLANNING AND SCHEDULING

1. Planning and scheduling must be performed in a formal, complete and consistent way. The customer–provided Project/Master Schedule, and all related subordinate schedules through the CA/WP levels, provide a logical sequence from summary to detailed Work Package activities.

The Earned Value approach serves as the "integrator" to make Work Package schedules compatible with contract and project milestones, since the integrated logic networks (PERT/CPM) are built from the Work Package data base.

2. Integrated Logic Network or Precedence Diagram Method (PDM) must be established for all interfaces within the logic framework of the Project Work Breakdown Structure (PWBS).

3. The Responsibility Assignment Matrix (RAM) is an output of WBS planning. It extends to specific levels in support of internal and customer reports. The RAM merges the WBS with the Organizational Breakdown Structure (OBS) to display the intersection of WBS on the vertical axis with CA responsible organizations shown on the horizontal axis (See Figure 1).

4. When Work Package Plans are detailed, the lowest level Work Packages are interfaced and scheduled with milestones (objective indicators) for measuring progress.

COMMON SENSE

No one ever said using Earned Value in a high–tech, product development or service enhancement environment would be easy. After all, it's not about building widgets. Care must be taken to determine and use the most efficient work planning and subsequent progress measuring techniques (objective indicators) possible. Herein lies the key to achieving a value added implementation of the Earned Value concept. Subjective estimates of percent complete will leave the user far short of realizing the process' potential.

The Work Packages are usually identified as either:

- Discrete Effort (DE): Effort which can be scheduled in relation to clearly definable start and completion dates, and which contains objective indicators against which performance can be measured.
- Level–of–Effort (LOE): Support effort that is not easily measured in terms of discrete accomplishment. LOE is characterized by a uniform rate of activity over a specific period of time.

Note: Where possible, categorize Work Packages in terms of discrete effort. Use of LOE should be minimized (10% maximum)

5. Schedule—General Characteristics

- Schedules shall be closely coordinated with all performing functional organizations (resource pools).
- Commitment to lower level schedules provides the basis for the scheduled baselines.
- All WP schedules are directly identifiable to a specific Control Account and WBS element and all Work Packages must appear in a vertically integrated schedule (Figure 4).

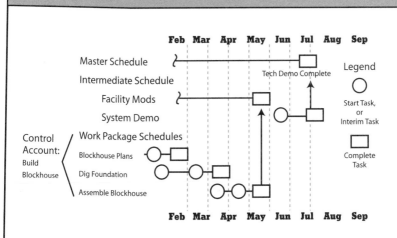

Vertically Integrated Schedule

Figure 4

• After a performance measurement baseline has been established, schedule dates must remain under strict revision control, changing only with the appropriate approval.

Exception: Non critical path Work Packages will have some flexibility as a result of their float.

6. Project Schedules—two distinct categories of schedules are used:

• Project Level Schedules are either Master Phasing/Milestone Program Schedules, WBS Intermediate Schedules or Control Account Schedules.

• Detailed Schedules are either Control Account Schedules or Work Package Schedules.

• Control Account Schedules:

1) Have milestones applicable to responsible organizations.

2) Are developed by the organizations to extend interfaces to lower Work Package items.

3) Are one level above the Work Package where status is normally determined and reported monthly to the project level for updating of higher level schedule status and performance measurement.

4) Have planned and authorized Work Packages which correlate with the CA, WBS, Scope of Work (SOW), and with reports to the customer.

5) Documents the schedule baseline for the project.

• Work Project Schedules:

1) Provide milestones (objective indicators) and activities required to identify performance against specific

measurable tasks.

2) Supply the framework for establishing and time phasing detailed budgets, various status reports, and summary of cost and schedule performance information.

3) Are the level at which Work Package status is normally discussed and provide input for performance measurement, forecasts and corrective actions.

4) Are the responsibility of a single performing organization (individual, if possible).

COMMON SENSE

Remember, because of other high priority project work and the resulting heavy demand on resources, you may not get that Subject Matter Expert (SME) you planned. Carefully assess and communicate how the work package plan is impacted by this "switch" in resource and/or its associated skill set differential.

RESOURCE POOL

5) Provide a schedule baseline against which each measurable WP must be identified.

6) Require formal authorization for changes after work has started, and normally provide a minimum of three months detail visibility.

7) Schedule Change Control

• The CAMs can commit their organization to a revised schedule only after formal approval.

COMMON SENSE

Don't forget, once the work packages are defined and scheduled the most important task for the Project Manager is to inform the Functional/Line manager who owns the resource(s) of the project's precise resource requirements AND get their commitment as to skill set capability potential and specific availability to support the specific project schedule.

8) Work Package Schedule Statusing

> • Objective indicators or milestones are used to identify measurable intermediate outputs and to support effective communication.

• Milestone schedule status and Budgeted Cost of Work Performed (BCWP) calculations are normally performed at this level monthly (users and/or organizations can specify reporting frequency).

MILESTONES/OBJECTIVE INDICATORS WILL IMPROVE COMMUNICATIONS

BUDGETING

In accordance with the Scope of Work (SOW) and/or Performance Requirements negotiated by the organization with the customer, the budgets for elements of work are allocated to the CAM through the Earned Value process. These budgets are tied to the Work Package plans, which have been approved in the PMB. The following top–down outline gives the CAM an overview of the total Earned Value budgeting process.

CREATING A PROJECT BUDGET

1. Project-to-Function Budgeting (Matrix Assignments)

- Budget Allocation

    1) The PM releases WBS Targets to WBS managers, who negotiate Control Account Targets with CAMs. The CAMs provide Work Package time phased planning.

    2) When all project effort is time phased and approved The Performance Measurement Baseline (PMB) is established.

    3) The time phased Work Package budgets (PV) are the basis for calculating Budgeted Cost of Work Performed (BCWP).

- Budget Adjustments

    1) The PMB can be changed with the PM's approval when either of the following occurs:

    - Changes in SOW (additions or deletions) cause adjustment to budgets.

• Formal rebaselining results in a revised total allocation of budget.

2. PMB budgets may not be replanned for changes in schedule (neither acceleration nor slips) or cost over/underruns.

3. Management Reserve (MR)

 • MR is budget set aside to cover unforeseen unanticipated "in scope" requirements.
 • A Work Package Change Record (WPCR) or equivalent is used to authorize add/delete transactions to the MR budget.

4. Undistributed Budget (UB)

 • UB is budget set aside to cover "identified, in-scope effort that is not yet detailed or assigned." As these efforts are assigned they are incorporated into the detail Work Package planning.

5. Detailed Planning

 • The Authorized Work Packages (AWP) and the Planned Work Package (PWP) comprise the budget (BCWS) within a CA.

COST ACCUMULATION

Cost Accumulation provides the CAM with a working knowledge of the Accounting methods used in Earned Value.

COMMON SENSE

The biggest challenge facing those organizations considering the use of Earned Value may be the lack of the necessary timely and/or accurate financial accounting information to supply the important AC data element. To date, accrual accounting (keeping your own set of project books) has been the only sure way to overcome this problem. Until an organization's accounting systems are enhanced and integrated with the Earned Value approach, accrual accounting may be the only viable option available to the Project Manager "committed" to Earned Value.

ACCOUNTING FOR ACTUAL COSTS

1. Labor Costs

- Timekeeping/cost collection for labor costs uses a labor distribution/accumulation system. The system shows monthly (or other) expenditure data based on labor charges against internal uniquely identified (numbered) Work Packages.

Note: Purchased/leased labor typically is accounted for as a "material" or non-labor cost.

2. Non-Labor Cost

- The Material Cost Collection Accounting shows monthly (or other) expenditure data based on purchase order/subcontract expenditure.
- The Subcontract/Integrated Contractor Cost Accounting uses reports received from the external sources for monthly expenditures.
- The Funds Control System (Commitments) records the total value of purchase orders/ subcontracts issued, but not totally funded. The cumulative dollar value of outstanding orders is reduced as procurements are funded.

3. The Accounting Charge Number System:

   • The accounting system typically uses two address numbers for charges to work packages:

   1) The Work Package number that consists of WBS —functional organization—CA—Work Package (others may be desired–Figure 5). 2) The combined Work Package Account Number, may consist of a single character ledger, 3-digit major account, and a 5-digit subaccount number.

   • Work Package charge numbers are authorized by a managers release of an AWP.

4. Accounting Charge Number composition (varies with organization)

   • Internal charge numbers
   (example 181-008-1-01)
   • External charge numbers are alphabetized Work Package numbers
   (example 186-005-2-AB)

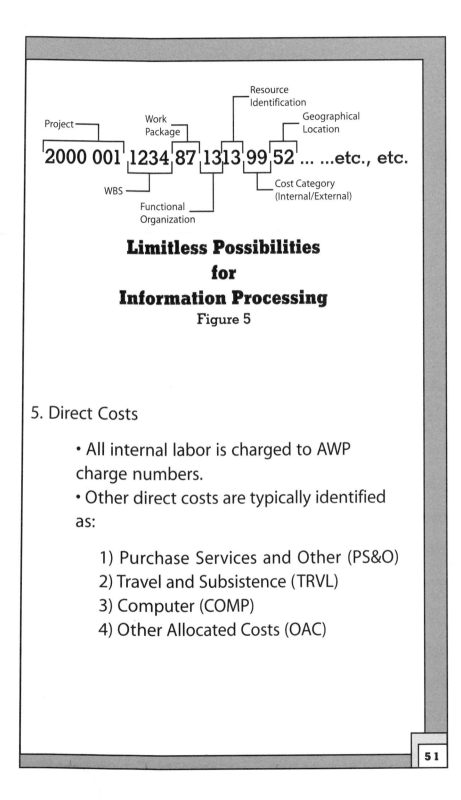

Project ── Work Package ── Resource Identification ── Geographical Location

2000 001 1234 87 1313 99 52 ... ...etc., etc.

WBS ── Functional Organization ── Cost Category (Internal/External)

Limitless Possibilities
for
Information Processing
Figure 5

5. Direct Costs

- All internal labor is charged to AWP charge numbers.
- Other direct costs are typically identified as:

    1) Purchase Services and Other (PS&O)
    2) Travel and Subsistence (TRVL)
    3) Computer (COMP)
    4) Other Allocated Costs (OAC)

6. Indirect Costs (Elements defined by organization)

- Indirect costs are charged to allocation pools, and distributed to internal Work Packages—or may be charged as actuals to Work Packages.
- Controllable labor overhead functions may be budgeted to separate Work Packages for monthly analysis of applied costs.

COMMON SENSE

Actual cost categories and accounting system address numbers will vary significantly depending on the organization. Extreme care must be taken to integrate Earned Value cost information requirements with other critical management information processes within the specific organization, i.e.; Cost Estimating System, MRP, Procurement/ Subcontracting, etc., if an Enterprise Application is to be achieved.

CHAPTER 3

PERFORMANCE MEASUREMENT

Performance Measurement for the CAM consists of requesting and evaluating Work Package status, with all EV calculated or determined at the WP level. Comparison of planned value (PV) versus Earned Value (EV) is made to obtain Schedule Variance (SV), and comparison of EV to actual cost (AC) is made to obtain cost variance (CV). Performance Measurement provides a vital input for management decisions.

1. Performance Measurement provides:

- Work progress status— what's been accomplished.
- Relationship of planned cost and schedule to actual accomplishment.
- Valid, timely, auditable data.
- Basis for Estimate at Completion(EAC), or Latest Revised Estimate (LRE).
- Summaries developed at the lowest practical WBS and organizational level.

2. Cost and Schedule Performance Measurement provides:

- Elements required to measure project progress and status are:

  1) WP schedule/Work Accomplished Status.
  2) Planned Value of Work Scheduled (PV).
  3) Value of Work Performed or Earned Value. (EV)
  4) Actual Cost for Work Performed (AC) or recorded or accrued cost.

- The sum of AWP and PWP budget values (PV) should equal CA budget value.
- Development of budgets provides these capabilities:

  1) Capability to plan and control cost.
  2) Capability to identify incurred costs for actual Work Package accomplishments and work in progress.
  3) Cost Account/ Work Package BCWP Measurement Levels.

3. Project Budgets establish the importance of:

- Measurable work and related event status form the basis for determining progress status for EV calculations.
- EV measurements at summary WBS levels result from accumulating the EV at the CA level.

Note: Within each CA the inclusion of LOE is kept to a minimum to prevent distortion of the total EV

- Some calculation methods used for measuring WP performance are:

    1) Short Work Packages are less than 3 months long. Their Earned Value (EV) equals PV up to a 80% limit of (PV) until the WP is completed.

    2) Long Work Packages exceed 3 months, and use Objective Indicator (OI) milestones. The Earned Value (EV) equals PV up to the month-end prior to the first incomplete OI.

    3) Level-of-Effort: Value (EV) is earned through passage of time and is equal to PV.

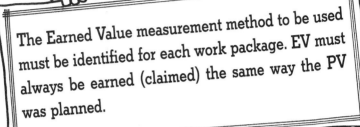

COMMON SENSE

The Earned Value measurement method to be used must be identified for each work package. EV must always be earned (claimed) the same way the PV was planned.

4. Estimate to Completion (ETC) Preparation considers:

- Cumulative actuals/commitments
- Remaining CA budget
- Labor sheets and grade/levels (Rates)
- Schedule status
- Previous ETC
- EV to date
- Cost improvements
- Historical data
- Future actions
- Approved changes

Earned Value "Claiming" Techniques
(Optional Methods of Establishing PV and Calculating EV)

0/100   Take all EV credit for performing work when the Work Package is complete.

50/50   Take EV credit for performing one–half of the work at the start of the Work Package; take EV credit for performing the remaining one–half when the Work Package is complete (Don't use this method on "long" Work Packages).

DISCRETE VALUE MILESTONES Divide work into separate, measurable activities. As the milestone is accomplished it earns the EV equal to PV planned for performing each activity during the time period it is completed.

EQUIVALENT UNITS If there are numerous similar items to complete, assume each is worth an equivalent portion of the total Work Package Value; take credit for performance according to the number of items completed during the period (i.e., widget count).

PERCENT COMPLETE Associate estimated percentages of Work Package completion with specific time periods; take EV credit for performance. If possible, use physical inspection to confirm percentages have been achieved (Avoid this approach, it is too subjective—*last 20% takes 80% of time).*

MODIFIED MILESTONE PERCENT COMPLETE Combines the discrete value milestone (objective indicator) and percent complete technique by allowing some "subjective estimate" of work accomplishment and EV credit for the associated "Earned Value" during reporting periods where no discrete milestone (OI) has been completed. The subjective earning of value for uncompleted milestone work is usually limited to one reporting period or up to 80% of the value of the scheduled discrete milestone. No additional Earned Value can be claimed until the preceding scheduled discrete milestone is completed (the most flexible approach–see Figure 6).

EARNED VALUE – HOW YOU GET IT

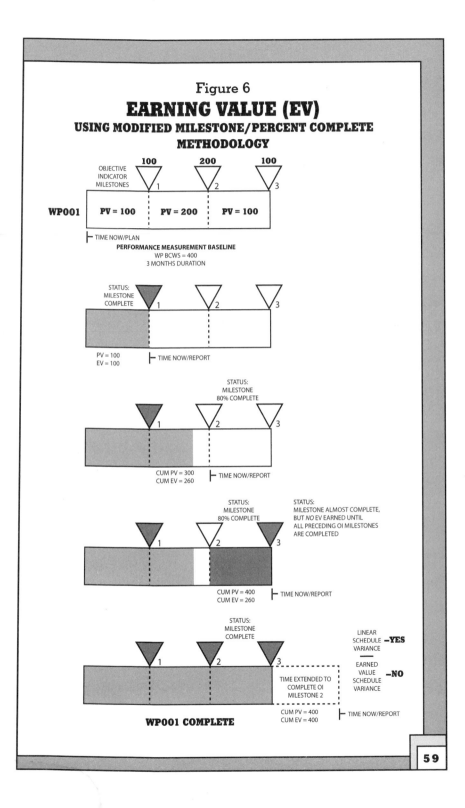

Figure 6
EARNING VALUE (EV)
USING MODIFIED MILESTONE/PERCENT COMPLETE METHODOLOGY

Based on a planned amount of support effort, assign value per period; take EV credit for performance based on passage of time (limited to 10% of total Work Package budgets).

APPORTIONED Milestones are developed as a percentage of a controlling discrete Work Package; credit for performance is taken upon completion of a related discrete milestone.

EARNED VALUE FOR HIGH TECHNOLOGY PROJECTS: AN INNOVATIVE APPROACH

High technology projects, with substantial "R" content, have often found the use of the traditional dollar, or cost, based Earned Value techniques too cumbersome, too restrictive, and considerably less than effective. Despite this relatively bad experience with EV on R&D projects, there is a modified EV approach that has demonstrated the capability to provide realistic, accurate and timely technology–based decision support information for R&D project managers and WBS managers, without relying on dollars as the primary data element.

This creative, technology–driven approach relies on developing and combining three independent "point value" data elements to generate the project's technical performance measurement baseline (PMB). The three critical components of the R&D EV methodology are (1) the position of each project Work Package on the precedence diagram/ critical path schedule, (2) the technical difficulty of each specific project WP as assessed by the individual contributor responsible for achieving the assigned technical objective; and (3) the level of risk (uncertainty) for each WP as it related to the successful and timely completion of the project, as assessed by the managers of the respective technical expertise areas involved.

The allocation of the total "EV points" (aka, PV) for any task is determined based on the following criteria:

To establish any task's EV point value, the formula is very simple: $F1(F2 + F3) = $ EV points. Using this formula, the maximum point value for any one task is 300 EV points, and the minimum for any one task is 10 EV points (Figure 7).

Figure 7

F1 – Value determined by on/off project critical path

WP Schedule Position	EV Rating (Points)
• On Critical Path (CP)	30
• $\leq$ 10 Days Off CP	25
• $\geq$ 11 Days Off CP	15
• $\geq$ 30 Days Off CP	10

F2 – Value determined by the project type and the assessed level of technical difficulty

EV Rating (Points)

• TYPE I
Pure Research
(Concept)

Very high levels of uncertainty of this project type result in very little value–added from using EV. Not recommended

• TYPE II
Development
(Post Research)

3–5 Based on technical difficulty (greater the difficulty, higher the value)

• TYPE III
Enhancement/
Improvement
(upgrade)

1–3 Based on technical difficulty (greater the difficulty, higher the value)

F3 – Value determined by assessing each work package to evaluate any risk factors that could impact the project.

EV Rating (Points)

• ALL PROJECT WP's

0–5 Based on assigned **WP** manager's level of confidence that the risk can be mitigated (greater the confidence, lower the value)

When the proper EV point values have been determined for each WP, the EV point values are assigned to the calendar time frame in which the WP is scheduled to be completed. It should be noted that since EV is awarded only when a WP is completed the shorter the individual task duration, the less distortion of the plan-to-actual comparison database. Subjectively determined EV "progress points" can be awarded as work proceeds, but this "percent complete" is not recommended unless the use of objective indicator milestones are incorporated into the plan. Once all WP EV point values have been properly assigned to a planned completion time, a project PMB curve (similar to a cumulative cost curve) is generated as the basis for variance analysis.

Note: Specifically tailored variance analysis reporting thresholds must be developed when utilizing this EV methodology.

As technical WPs are completed, EV points are earned. The total EV points for the current reporting period, or the total for the cumulative-to-date period, can be determined and then compared to the expected achievement EV point value represented by the PMB. These EV point plan-to-actual comparisons can be generated and analysis conducted for the project total or any subdivision of the total R&D project, i.e., by individual WP, by technology or functional group, by product component, or even by an individual responsible researcher/technical contributor.

This unique application of EV to R&D oriented projects provides management information that is, by its very derivation, clearly consistent with planned technical work and the work that has actually been accomplished. Obviously, the EV integration of planned effort and actual accomplishment relies heavily on candid input during planning and progress reporting by the project management professional. The R&D project manager serves as the catalyst for the development of the EV point data and as a coordinator and/or integrator of the EV data at the various project summary levels.

To realize the full range of benefits from this EV point approach, it is imperative that the WBS is properly structured and carefully numbered to facilitate the many different "information sorts" needed to support the project management decision making process throughout the life of the project.

VARIANCE ANALYSIS

If Performance Measurement gives results in schedule or cost variances in excess of pre–established control zone thresholds, analyses must be conducted to determine the cause and effect. The CAM is mainly concerned with variances that exceed thresholds established for the Control Account. Analyses of these variances provide "opportunities" to identify and resolve problems or opportunities at all project levels.

COMMON SENSE

During variance analysis always compare a minimum of three data points to confirm status, i.e., cost, schedule, manpower, and/or materials. Consistent data quickly directs you to the probable cause. Inconsistent data suggests need for further analysis and investigation as to the root cause of the variance—**the truth**.

1. Preparation

• The cost–oriented variance analysis should include a review of cumulative and at–completion cost data. Reports should exhibit cost variances (CV) and schedule variances (SV) dollar (or other quantities) differences at the CA plan summary level.

• The calendar–schedule linear analysis should include a review of the status of any milestones that impact critical dates or exceed available float on the non–critical paths.

• Variances are identified to the CA level during this stage of the review.

• Both CV and SV are developed for current period and cumulative–to–date as well as at–completion status.

• Determination is made whether a variance impact is cost or schedule–oriented or both.

• Variance Analysis Reports (VAR) are developed on significant (exceeds control zone thresholds–see Figure 9) CA variances.

COMMON SENSE

In Earned Value, variances from the Performance Measurement Baseline (PMB) with a (-) are considered bad (behind schedule or over cost per work unit output) and those with a (+) are deemed good (ahead of schedule or under cost per work unit output). Technically, there are no good or bad variances. There are just variances, (difference between what you thought it would be and what it really is). Variances should be viewed as opportunities to understand the past, learn from it, and improve project performance in the future. But, remember, technically speaking, in Earned Value: (-) is bad, (+) is good.

2. Presentation of Findings

• Variance analyses should be prepared when one or more of the following exceed the thresholds established by the PM.

1) Schedule variance (EV - PV)
2) Cost variance (EV - AC)
3) At-completion variance (BAC - EAC or LRE)

See Figure 8 for variance examples.

Figure 8

INTERPRETATION OF SIMPLE
EARNED VALUE DATA CONDITIONS

PV	EV	AC	CONDITION
$100	$100	$100	On Schedule and On Cost
$200	$200	$100	On Schedule and Underrun
$100	$100	$200	On Schedule and Overrun
$100	$200	$200	Ahead of Schedule and On Cost
$100	$200	$100	Ahead of Schedule and Underrun
$100	$200	$300	Ahead of Schedule and Overrun
$200	$100	$100	Behind Schedule and On Cost
$300	$200	$100	Behind Schedule and Underrun
$200	$100	$300	Behind Schedule and Overrun

SAMPLE LOGIC AND DATA CONSISTENCY CHECKS

LOGIC CHECK	EXPLANATION
CURRENT EV/PV RATIO (SPI) INDICATES POOR PLANNING	The amount of work performed during the reporting period was less than half the amount of work scheduled
CURRENT EV/AC RATIO (CPI) INDICATES POOR EARNING METHOD	The actual cost of the work performed during the reporting period was less than half the budgeted cost for such work
CUMMULATIVE PV WITH NO CUMULATIVE EV	No work has been performed to date, in a category for which work was scheduled in this or an earlier reporting period
AC INCREASE WITHOUT EV INCREASE	Cost has increased without work being performed (may indicate rework or technical problems have occurred)
AC CHARGES TO UNOPENED WORK PACKAGE	WP has not started; therefore, no cost should be charged
BAC OR PV INCONSISTENCY DATA SHOULD BE CORRECTED	Cumulative time–phased budget assigned to WP cannot be greater than total budgeted value
BAC/LRE OR AC INCONSISTENCY–DATA SHOULD BE CORRECTED	Money spent to date cannot exceed the total amount to be spent for WP's
BAC/LRE POSSIBLE INCONSISTENCY–EAC/LRE DOES NOT REFELECT CUM. COST OVERRUN	Indicated cost is unrealistic when compared to performance data

COMMON SENSE

Remember, be thorough in your variance analysis. Do not "jump" to conclusions. Evaluate the conditions and causes carefully. The corrective action must be thoroughly examined. Adding more people is not always the answer. There is a point of diminishing returns. Can nine women produce a baby in one month?

In other words…

THIS SHOULD STOP THE SCHEDULE SLIP! LET ME KNOW IF YOU NEED MORE

RESOURCES

PM

BOSS

IS MORE BETTER?

3. Operation

- Internal analysis reports will document variances that exceed thresholds (Figure 9). Schedule Problem Analysis Reports (SPAR's) for "time-based" linear schedule, or CA Variance Analysis Reports (CA VAR) for dollarized cost/schedule variances will be prepared.
- Analysis and explanations are submitted to the customer when agreed thresholds are exceeded.
- Emphasis will be placed upon corrective action for resolution of variant conditions.
- Corrective action will be assigned to specific individuals and tracked for effectiveness and completion (action items).
- Internal project variance analyses and corrective action shall be formally reviewed in regular management meetings.
- Informal reviews of cost and schedule variance analysis data may occur daily, weekly, or monthly depending on the nature and severity of the variance.

ESTABLISHING AND COMMUNICATING EARNED VALUE REPORTING THRESHOLDS

(Current Period and/or Cumulative–to–date)

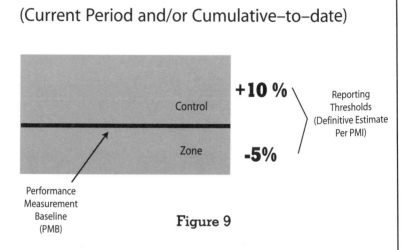

Figure 9

Each project should establish its own Earned Value "control zone" thresholds consistent with the organization's criteria, project type, complexity, urgency and precision of the Performance Measurement Baseline being measured. Definitive estimates provide +10%, -5% levels of precision. Budget estimates provide +25%, -10% levels of precision. Control zones with thresholds inconsistent with the estimate or project type will result in excess (and potentially non–productive) variance reporting.

Proper implementation of the Earned Value control zone thresholds will minimize the micro management, while constantly focusing management attention on the more significant project variances thus facilitating proactive decision making. Typically, formal project reporting is accomplished one level above the lowest level of planning (Work Package). The control zone thresholds are enforced at this level.

Variances within the control zone must be recognized, reviewed and thoroughly understood by the assigned responsible project participant, but no "formal" or documented report is required. Variances outside the control zone must be thoroughly examined to determine: cause, impact (if any) and corrective action (if any). Specific findings and subsequent actions taken require appropriate documentation.

Note: Always compare a minimum of three data points. Schedule, cost, and manpower utilization. Consistent data makes analysis easy. Inconsistant data points to potential problems.

COMMON SENSE

Don't get too myopic when considering Earned Value Schedule Variances (EV-PV). Remember the Earned Value SV often times may result from slow accomplishment rates on Work Packages "off" the critical path. In this case you may have an Earned Value SV, but the project's delivery date may not be affected. In other words, you are using float! But the critical path integrity is not compromised. It is imperative that you carefully integrate the Earned Value SV with the linear time schedule established through the use of an integrated logic precedence diagram (Pert/CPM).

Some project managers or organizations may also require that an "absolute $$$ value" be included as part of the control zone along with the standard % designation. If this approach is used, both thresholds must be exceeded before formal reporting is necessary. This dual threshold technique is almost always used in "official" government implementations of EVMS.

PROJECT REPORTING

There are two basic report categories: customer (external) and internal. Customer performance reports are usually contractually established with specific, fixed content and timing. Internal reports support the projects with the data that relates to lower organizational and WBS levels. The CAM is mainly concerned with these lower level reports.

1. Customer Reporting (when required)

- A customer requires summary level reporting, typically on a monthly basis.
- The customer examines the detailed data for areas that may include a significant (out of control zone threshold) variance.
- The Cost Performance Report (CPR) is the Earned Value vehicle used to accumulate and report cost and schedule performance data.

2. In-house Reporting

- Internal management practices emphasize assignment of responsibility for internal reports to an individual CAM.
- Reporting formats reflect past and current performance, and the forecast level of future performance (See Figure 10).

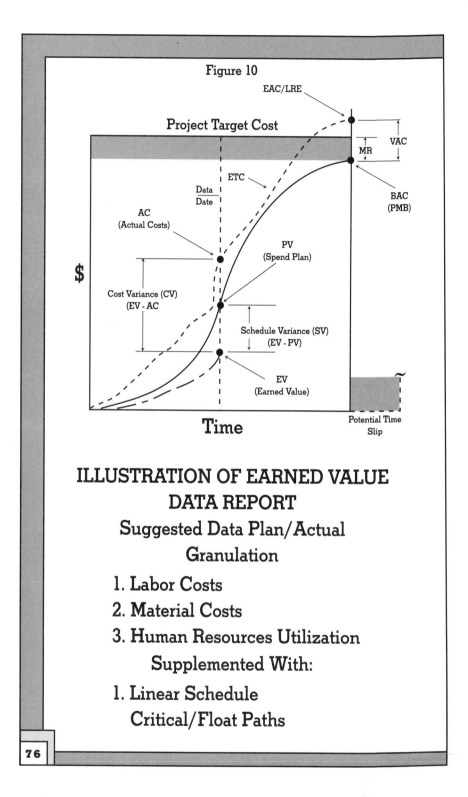

Figure 10

ILLUSTRATION OF EARNED VALUE
DATA REPORT
Suggested Data Plan/Actual
Granulation

1. Labor Costs
2. Material Costs
3. Human Resources Utilization
   Supplemented With:

1. Linear Schedule
   Critical/Float Paths

• Performance review meetings are held:

1) Monthly for cost and schedule (more frequently as required).
2) As needed for review of problem areas.

• The CAM emphasizes cumulative to–date and to–go cost, schedule, and human resource utilization on the CA Work Packages

1) It is primarily at the Work Package level that review of performance (EV), actuals (AC), and budget (PV) is coupled with objective performance influenced judgement(performance indices) to determine the ETC.
2) The CAM is responsible for the accuracy and completeness of the revised estimates and supporting forecasts and trend analysis.

CHAPTER 4

ONCE YOU HAVE THE DATA, WHAT CAN YOU DO WITH IT?

Remember, Work Package level planning and statusing has been emphasized due to their significance in the Earned Value approach. Specifically, for establishing/maintaining the relevance and integrity of the project information, thus enhancing the ability of the user to successfully deliver on the project's triple constraint.

The following definitions are provided in "lay" terms to facilitate understanding.

VARIANCE TYPES

Cost Variance (CV) or budgeted value* for work performed minus actual cost incurred to perform the work that has been completed.

$$EV - AC = CV$$

---

* What you plan to spend to get the work done (typical wherever the term value is used).

Schedule Variances (SV) or budgeted value* of work performed minus budget estimated for work scheduled to be done.

$$EV - PV = SV$$

Variance at Completion (VAC) or original budget estimated for all work planned minus new budget estimate for all work (done and remaining to be done) based on past performance and other known factors.

$$BAC - EAC \text{ or } LRE = VAC$$

PERFORMANCE INDICES

Cost Performance Index (CPI) or budgeted value of the work performed divided by the actual cost incurred to perform the work that has been completed.

$$\frac{EV}{AC} = CPI$$

Schedule Performance Index (SPI) or budgeted value of the work performed divided by budgeted value for the estimated work schedule to be done.

$$\frac{EV}{PV} = SPI$$

---

* What you plan to spend to get the work done (typical wherever the term value is used).

To Complete Performance Index (TCPI) or original budget estimate for all work planned minus budgeted value for the work performed. That quantity divided by the original budget estimate for all work planned minus actual cost incurred to perform the work that has been completed to-date.

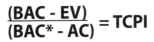

$$\frac{(BAC - EV)}{(BAC^* - AC)} = TCPI$$

*if known EAC or LRE may be substituted for BAC to include effect of performance to–date

EV Schedule Conversions to Time or Original budget estimate for all work planned divided by SPI minus original budget estimate for all work planned. That quantity is divided by average time period (days, weeks or months) budget estimate for work scheduled to be done to–date.

$$\frac{(BAC/SPI) - BAC}{AVG. PV^{**}} = SV \text{ (linear time)}$$

**Avg. time period BCWS may be calculated using the project days, weeks, months to–date or a selected number of recent days, weeks, or months.

These EV Performance data are extremely important in understanding the current status of a project and perhaps more importantly they are critical in predicting what the future status of the project could be.

The concept of Performance Indices (PI) allows the users to get to the "truth" about future project performance possibilities. In other words, the Project Manager concocts his/her own version of Sodium Pentothal (truth serum) by using these Performance Indices to confirm what level of performance will be needed to complete a project as planned.

Using PI, the absolute value of 1 is the planned expectation. Less than 1 is poorer performance than planned and greater than 1 is better performance than planned. These factors apply in Cost and Schedule alike.

Therefore, if a performer reported an SPI of .67, but advised you the performance would be back at 1 next period, you should be wary. Request an explanation of how this dramatic performance adjustment will be achieved. You could calculate the TCPI to determine just how dramatic the improvement will need to be.

If you're lucky the performer **will have a plan**, if not, one will be needed. This approach eliminates the personal subjectiveness of variances and projections and focuses on the work content and what must be done if recovery is to be accomplished. If the PIs fall below .5, chances of recovery are questionable, unless the data is generated very early in the project. (Although the DOD suggests this forecasting is meaningful after as little at 15% of the project is complete—most project managers agree that >30% is far more realistic).

It's a fact! You can count on it! It has been proven that on most projects whatever happened in the past will continue to happen in the future—**unless someone does something about it**. This forecasting or predicting is founded in the "truth" of past performance and is at the heart of the objective to change project management from a reactive process to a proactive process. **Result**: users identify and manage potentially serious project problems, while they are still small and capable of being solved in a timely and cost–effective manner.

OTHER USEFUL EV DATA

STATUS AS % OF PLAN:

% Complete or budget value of work done/(time now) divided by the original budget estimated at completion for all work planned, then multiply by 100:

$$\frac{EV}{BAC} \times 100 = \% \text{ Complete}$$

% Spent or actual cost incurred for work done (time now) divided by the original budget estimated at completion for all work planned, then multiply by 100.

$$\frac{AC}{BAC} \times 100 = \% \text{ Spent}$$

ESTIMATE TO COMPLETE

ETC or original budget value at completion for all work planned minus budgeted value of the work done divided by the CPI.

$$\frac{(BAC - EV)}{CPI} = ETC$$

ESTIMATE AT COMPLETION/LATEST REVISED ESTIMATE

CUMULATIVE CPI METHOD

$$\frac{BAC}{CPI} = EAC$$

3 MONTH AVERAGE METHOD

$$AC + \left(\frac{EV\ 3\ \text{MONTHS}}{AC\ 3\ \text{MONTHS}} \right)^{(BAC - EV)} = EAC$$

COST/SCHEDULE WEIGHTED FACTOR METHOD

$$EAC = AC + \frac{(BAC - EV)}{(.8CPI + .2SPI)}$$

COST/SCHEDULE METHOD*

$$AC + \frac{(BAC - EV)}{(CPI \times SPI)} = EAC$$

*Considered to be "worst case"

MATERIAL (VENDORS, CONTRACTORS, PURCHASES, LEASES, ETC.) PLANNING AND ACCOUNTING OPTIONS TO CONSIDER FOR "EARNING VALUE" METHOD

Point of Order = Plan for, estimate, and record costs at the time material is ordered.

Point of Receipt = Plan for, estimate, and record costs at the time material is received.

Point of Usage = Plan for, estimate, and record costs at the time material is used.

MATERIAL PRICE AND USAGE VARIANCES

Usage Variance = (planned quantity minus actual quantity) multiply by planned price.

Price Variance = (planned price minus actual price) multiply by actual quantity.

To assure value added use of Earned Value, a great deal of thought should be given to the material planning and accounting topic. Done poorly, this element alone can distort the project management information until it becomes very disconnected from the realities of the project and therefore causes serious question as to the value. First, make an early decision regarding how you will account for materials and secondly, seriously consider separating materials from labor for planning and tracking purposes See Page 86).

CHAPTER 5

TRAIN THE USERS

User training is a critical element in the effective use of an Earned Value approach to project management. Those organizations that have invested the time to create and deliver the small amount of training necessary to spread the knowledge of Earned Value methods throughout their management structure have clearly realized substantial benefits.

Comprehensive "real world" training should result in "real world" learning. In all cases the training must be developed around an organization's policy for utilizing Earned Value. Each company will have slightly different requirements and implementation objectives. A "generic" training course is of limited value unless the attendees can easily adapt and apply what has been learned to the specific requirements of their organization.

THE TEACHER'S CHALLENGE

$$SV = EV - PV$$
$$CV = EV - AC$$

Does this apply to me?

A well conceived, properly developed, and professionally delivered training program will achieve the desired results and will assist users in realizing the most productive and cost-effective use of the powerful Earned Value project management approach.

COMMON SENSE

Remember, providing Earned Value training doesn't necessarily mean you have provided Earned Value **learning**. Post-training mentoring and follow-up will be the key to converting an interesting theory to applied reality.

MENTORING: THE UP–CLOSE AND PERSONAL APPROACH TO LEARNING

Almost all forms of training produce some learning. Seminars with live instructors; on–line curriculum with "invisible" instructor resources; CD's with all the fancy bells and whistles; and specially developed books and manuals all provide different approaches and a variety of opportunities for students to learn.

However, nothing enhances the learning process more than good old–fashioned On–Job Training (OJT)—especially when it is combined with a well designed mentoring or coaching approach. None of the other training methodologies come close to enabling the new "students" to achieve the quantity and quality of knowledge transfer that is realized as a result of this mentoring process.

Mentors, although usually subject matter experts, must be carefully chosen. They **must** have the depth and breadth of knowledge in the specific application area AND they must be willing and able to share their intellectual property with their "students" in an open and non–threatening way. When it comes to learning the realities of a beneficially applied project management, a qualified and enthusiastic mentor is worth their weight in gold. Mentors are the common denominator in the formula for converting PM academic theory to organizational applied reality.

CHAPTER 6

THINKING ABOUT USING PROJECT MANAGEMENT? THINK ABOUT THIS

Successful project management systems don't happen by accident. You have to get off on the right foot. Evaluating software packages for supporting the PM process is one of the first steps you'll have to take; hopefully, these thoughts will help you get started.

THE ROLE OF PROJECT MANAGEMENT APPLICATIONS TODAY

Timely strategic and tactical decisions are key to the future success of any company. These decisions depend on decision makers getting the right information at the right time. Delivering timely information within the context of a dynamic, on-going project has always been a major challenge for most corporate information systems.

But it is exactly this kind of challenge that has sparked the recent upsurge of interest in integrating project management tools into enterprise application suites. But, beware. It's a big job!

For many years full–scale implementations of project management software were confined to a relatively small number of companies working in the defense, aerospace, construction and petrochemical industries. Today, however, more and more corporations are transforming their internal structure by the increasing use of project–based teams that cut across traditional organizational hierarchies. From manufacturing plants to financial institutions, organizations consider the ability to plan, monitor, and report on projects a critical part of their business. And they're finding out that project management software can help them manage schedules, resources, and budgets, providing them with a vital business advantage.

For their part, project management software vendors have responded to new developments in enterprise-level software solutions by opening up their once proprietary data formats and making it easier for their products to interface with corporate data stored in a variety of formats. This has allowed project management functionality to be bundled into high-level application suites, even within organizations that previously had little experience with this type of tool.

At the same time, advances in graphical user interfaces and innovative training aids have succeeded in opening up powerful project management functionality to a much larger user population. Communication technologies such as email and the Internet now make it possible for project information to be instantly accessed and processed from even the most remote locations.

Clearly, the emergence of project management applications as mainstream business tools has elevated the importance of selecting the appropriate project management software. Once used primarily by a handful of schedulers and planners tucked away in a project control office, project management applications now collect and analyze information that has significant long–term business implications for many organizations.

Obviously, picking the right tool(s) is critical. The wide range of project management software vendors in today's marketplace makes it imperative that you develop a thorough and objective means for evaluating the various potential solutions.

How do you start?

As with any other project, if you do not plan the evaluation process you risk overlooking important activities, or performing the work out of sequence. This may result in adding time and cost to the project, or selecting a tool that does not meet your project management needs.

So, before you pick up the phone to start calling suppliers, take this time to map out the overall process of this evaluation effort. Start by considering the next two steps carefully:

1. COMMITTING TO THE EVALUATION PROCESS DELIVERABLE: PROJECT CHARTER

You've probably heard this already, but it bears repeating:

The evaluation and selection of a project management tool does not occur in a vacuum. In fact, the absence of management support for the evaluation effort is almost always the recipe for failure. Make sure everyone is "on board" before the "train" leaves the station.

Typically, the first step in planning your evaluation effort is determining the composition of the evaluating team, and having it help you determine the scope and duration of the evaluation project. When picking potential team members, start by considering your existing or intended users, provided that they have the necessary project management experience and knowledge. After all, if the users are part of the decision making process, successful and timely implementation of the selected software is more likely.

On the other hand, your intended users may require further training or experience before they can adequately judge the merits of competing solutions. In this event, you may want to include individuals outside of your user base who have the expertise to test and evaluate the software's capabilities.

You may also want to include other experts who have a strong interest in the functioning of your organization's project management system—accountants, for example, who will be relying on information about the planning of project budgets in order to estimate future cash flow. And you will almost certainly want to involve Information Systems experts who understand your company's long–range information strategies and goals. Make certain that all evaluators' time is blocked out for the duration of the evaluation effort. The lack of this resource commitment at a crucial point during the process can jeopardize even the best–organized evaluation effort.

If your company is like most others, tossing out a term like "resource commitments" is almost always guaranteed to get management's attention. It should! From the earliest stages of this process you'll need to have unequivocal support from your management about carrying out this effort—support that translates into people, time, and money. To help you win that support, it's always a good idea to have a documented analysis of why your current project management system is no longer adequate. Being able to identify this "point of pain" is often a crucial ingredient in getting management on board.

Why won't they listen: It's not just about software!!

In many organizations, this type of management signoff for the evaluation effort might take the form of a project charter, a formal document that reflects your organization's commitment to proceed. In other situations, a less formal authorization may suffice. In any case, what's important is that all parties understand the basic ground rules under which the evaluation process will occur, at least some notion of the costs involved, and a firm commitment to proceed.

2. CONDUCTING A NEEDS ASSESSMENT
DELIVERABLE: SCOPE DOCUMENT

How many times have you seen this happen? A survey form suddenly appears on your desk asking you to list the features you need from a certain type of software. Typically, the form consists of pages and pages of feature descriptions, and usually includes some type of rating system that allows you to prioritize desired features. Once you and your co-workers return the forms, the results are tabulated and then synthesized into a specification list to be passed on to potential vendors.

While these types of "bottom-up" surveys

certainly have their place in the evaluation process, experience shows that they are seldom a good place to start. Typically, the result is a long list of features that plunges the evaluation process into a mass of lower–level detail at a very early stage. Given the subjective nature of user surveys, this should not come as a surprise.

For example, assume that you've handed out surveys to three different types of users: team leaders, professional project schedulers, and upper–level executives. The team leaders might not know (or care) how project data is stored; they're simply interested in producing a standard barchart of their activities once a month. The master scheduler expects the system to be able to handle the calculation of a massive network that encompasses numerous subprojects, but is not all that concerned with the manual updating of progress information. Company executives aren't interested in the finer details of resource leveling algorithms; they simply want to be able to find out if their projects are on schedule.

When confronted with these three sets of responses to the survey, the person charged with summarizing the results has little choice but to compile a detailed list of features that may or may not be compatible with each other.

On the other hand, it is also possible for an important item to be not listed simply because it did not occur to any individual user. As a result, these types of lists may have serious omissions in functionality that will remain undetected until much later in the process.

A more successful approach to assessing needs might start with a bird's eye view of the project management process within the organization as a whole.

This means that a project management methodology that meets the company objectives and goals must be agreed to upfront. This is not always an easy task to accomplish, yet the effectiveness of both the evaluation effort and the eventual project management system implemented as the result of the evaluation effort, depend on it.

To arrive at an agreed–upon methodology, you might begin by breaking down your corporate requirements into broad categories that serve to maintain the focus on the highest level of system functionality, not the lowest. The following is a typical set of concerns that might be addressed during this stage of needs assessments:

Enterprise Issues:
How is project information integrated into the larger data environment of your organization? At what levels do projects need to be planned, tracked, and reported? What types of information are to be shared using the project management application? What standards need to be enforced to support this integration between projects? These types of questions require you to look at the project management function, not just in isolation, but in the larger context of your corporate data infrastructure.

Multi-User Access:
What are the roles of the users and their interaction with the system? For example, you may want one group of users to control all project data input and output except for progressing. If this is the case, then what level of access is required by other groups of users? Do users need to share data on a concurrent basis? Do multiple users need to be able to access the same project or auxiliary information simultaneously? The same activity record? Do not assume that just because an application can be installed on a local area network that users will have shared access or

concurrence beyond allowing two or more users access to the application. What about security?

Multi-Project Capabilities:
The term "multi-project" can mean different things to different people. Do you need the simple ability to break large projects into more manageable subprojects? Or do you require true multi-project scheduling features such as the ability to define interproject links, even at different levels of the project structures? Do you need to be able to perform resource scheduling across multiple projects so you can see the impact of resource limitations on a corporate-wide basis? What about cross-project reporting? How do you want to handle shared ancillary data such as code files?

Resource Management:
Is resource management a requirement of your organization? If it is, do you need to assign and schedule resources on a single project or across multiple projects? Do you need to manage resources on a single project or across multiple projects? Do you need to manage resources at a level higher than the individual resource (for example, by skill or by department)? What are the

budget implications of your resource assignments? Do you need to track actual costs tied directly to resources?

Open Architecture:
How will the project management application communicate with other corporate databases such as ERP, work authorization, or timesheet systems? For example, do you require an application that takes advantage of a client/server database architecture to update a corporate database through SQL transactions? Does it need to support OLE automation, which allows customization and integration with other applications? By insisting on an open architecture for the application, you are not only facilitating the eventual integration with your current data environment, you are protecting your future investment.

Earned Value:
Does your organization use an Earned Value approach that integrates schedule and cost controls for a project? Do you need to be able to manage and audit changes in the Performance Measurement Baseline? Do your projects require the tracking of costs using multiple currencies? Do you require special report formats for Earned Value information?

Project Management Methodology:
In many organizations, the output from a project management system is only part of a package of project–related deliverables that must be processed on a regular basis in a standardized format.

In this case, a requirement may exist for an automated process tool that allows you to integrate project management reports into other media, such as word processing documents, slide presentations, or email messages. You may also have a requirement for a process management tool if you have a set of standard operating procedures that are to be used with each project.

User Analysis:
Who will use the system and for what purpose? Remember that the typical large scale installation may include a wide range of users, from team leaders entering progress information to highly skilled schedulers who can take advantage of the most sophisticated project management functionality. Since such different groups of users are unlikely to have the

same level of experience working with project management software, some project management systems rest on data being moved back and forth among different applications, a daunting exercise in data integration. What may make more sense is a single product with a scalable interface that allows each user population to work with the appropriate level of functionality, while maintaining a single repository of project date.

Stakeholder Analysis:
In addition to the direct users of the software, other members of your organization are likely to have an interest in its functionality, from company executives in oversight positions to crew chiefs who are assigned work orders for their next day's work. Typically, you must analyze the scope, format, and level of detail needed for each type of report. You will also consider potential delivery systems such as email, the Internet, or corporate intranets.

Risk Analysis:
Another corporate need might be for a risk analysis feature that allows you to identify risk,

improve forecasts, and estimate the certainty with which key events can be predicted to occur as scheduled. This type of capability might be important in cases where an organization must decide whether to proceed with a contingency plan if the delay of the project seems likely.

Hardware/Software Environment:
Are you required to work within your current hardware environment, or are you budgeting for new equipment? If you are updating to new hardware platforms, when will these be available? Does the application need to work with an existing suite of software?

Once this type of needs analysis is complete, you should be able to summarize the results in a scope document that describes your corporate project management requirements. This document should reflect the overall parameters of the proposed project management functionality, as well as a relatively short list of key requirements that can serve as benchmarks for a successful implementation.

INDUSTRY STANDARD GUIDELINES FOR EARNED VALUE MANAGEMENT SYSTEMS (EVMS)

EVMS GUIDELINES

This section provides basic guidelines for companies to use in establishing and applying an integrated Earned Value Management System (EVMS). These guidelines are expressed in fundamental terms and provide flexibility for each company to optimize its system and be fully accountable for the effectiveness of its usage. The guidelines are grouped in five major categories as documented below. This information is supplemented with a glossary of common EVMS terminology.

1.1 Organization

   a. Define all authorized work elements for the project. A Work Breakdown Structure (WBS), tailored for effective internal management control, is commonly used in this process.

b. Identify the project Organizational Breakdown Structure (OBS) including the major subcontractors/vendors responsible for accomplishing the authorized work, and define the organizational elements in which work will be planned and controlled.

c. Provide for the integration of the company's planning, scheduling, budgeting, work authorization and cost accumulation processes with each other, and as appropriate, the project WBS and the project organizational structure OBS.

d. Identify the company organization or function responsible for controlling overhead (indirect costs).

e. Provide for integration of the project WBS and the project OBS in a manner that permits cost and schedule performance measurement by elements of either or both structures as needed.

1.2 Planning, Scheduling, and Budgeting

a. Schedule the authorized work in a manner which describes the sequence of work and identifies significant task interdependencies required to meet the requirements of the project.

b. Identify physical products, milestones, technical performance goals, or other indicators that will be used to measure progress.

c. Establish and maintain a time–phased budget baseline, at the control account level, against which project performance can be measured. Budget for far–term efforts may be held in higher level accounts until an appropriate time for allocation at the control account level. Initial budgets established for performance measurement will be based on either internal management goals or the external customer negotiated target cost including estimates for authorized, but undefinitized work.

Note: On government contracts, if an over target baseline is used for performance measurement reporting purposes, prior notification must be provided to the customer.

d. Establish budgets for authorized work with identification of significant cost elements (labor, material, etc.) as needed for internal management and for control of subcontractors/vendors.

e. To the extent it is practical to identify the authorized work in discrete work packages, establish budgets for this work in terms of dollars, hours, or other measurable units. Where the entire control account is not subdivided into work packages, identify the far term effort in larger planning packages for budget and scheduling purposes.

f. Provide that the sum of all work package budgets plus planning package budgets within a control account equals the control account budget.

g. Identify and control the level of effort (LOE) activity by time–phased budgets established for this purpose. Only that effort which is immeasurable or for which measurement is impractical may be classified as LOE.

h. Establish overhead budgets for each significant organizational component of the company for expenses which will become indirect costs.

Reflect in the project budgets, at the appropriate level, the amounts in overhead pools that are planned to be allocated to the project as indirect costs.

i. Identify management reserves and undistributed budget.

j. Provide that the project target cost goal is reconciled with the sum of all internal project budgets and management reserves.

1.3 Accounting Considerations

a. Record direct costs in a manner consistent with the budget in formal system controlled by the general book of accounts.

b. When a work breakdown structure is used, summarize direct costs from control accounts into the work breakdown structure without allocation of a single control account to two or more work breakdown structure elements.

c. Summarize direct costs from the control accounts into the appropriate organizational elements without allocation of a single control account to two or more organizational elements.

d. Record all indirect costs which will be allocated to the project.

e. Identify unit costs, equivalent unit costs, or "lot" costs when needed.

f. For EVMS, the material account system will provide for:

(1) Accurate cost accumulation and assignment of costs to control accounts in a manner consistent with the budgets using recognized, acceptable, costing techniques.

(2) Cost performance measurement at the point in time most suitable for the category of material involved, but no earlier than the time of progress payments or actual receipt of material.

(3) Full accountability of all material purchased for the project, including the residual inventory.

1.4 Analysis and Management Reports

a. At least on a monthly basis, generate the following information at the control account and other levels as necessary for management control using actual cost data from, or reconcilable with, the accounting system:

(1) Comparison of the amount of planned budget and the amount of budget earned for work accomplished. This comparison provides the schedule variance (SV).

(2) Comparison of the amount of the budget earned and the actual (applied where appropriate) direct costs for the same work. This comparison provides the cost variance (CV).

b. Identify, at least monthly, the significant differences between both planned and actual schedule performance and planned and actual cost performance, and provide the reasons for the variances in the detail needed by project management.

c. Identify budgeted and applied (or actual) indirect costs at the level and frequency needed by management for effective control, along with the reasons for any significant variances.

d. Summarize the data elements and associated variances through the project organization and/or work breakdown structure to support management needs and any customer reporting specified in the contract.

e. Implement managerial actions taken as the result of Earned Value information.

f. Develop revised estimates of cost at completion based on performance to date, commitment values for material, and estimates of future conditions.

Compare this information with the performance measurement baseline to identify variances at completion important to company management and any applicable customer reporting requirements including statements of funding requirements.

1.5 Revisions and Data Maintenance

a. Incorporate authorized changes in a timely manner, recording the effects of such changes in budgets and schedules. In the event of directed effort, prior to negotiation of a change, base such revisions on the amount estimated and budgeted to the project organizations.

b. Reconcile current budgets to prior budgets in terms of changes to the authorized work and internal replanning in the detail needed by management for effective control.

c. Control retroactive changes to records pertaining to work performed that would change previously reported amounts for actual costs, Earned Value, or budgets. Adjustments should be made only for correction of errors, routine accounting adjustments, effects of customer or management directed changes, or to improve the baseline integrity and accuracy of performance measurement data.

d. Prevent revisions to the project budget except for authorized changes.

e. Document changes to the Performance Measurement Baseline (PMB).

MORE INFORMATION:

1. **OSD Earned Value Management Home Page**
www.acq.osd.mil/pm

2. **Defense Contract Management Command (DCMC) Earned Value Management Implementation Guide**
www.ntsc.navy.mil/Resources/Library/Acqguide/evmig.doc

3. **Industry Standard Guidelines for Earned Value Management Systems**
www.ntsc.navy.mil/Resources/Library/Acqguide/evms_gde.doc

4. **Earned Value Data Analysis** www.nnh.com/ev/var2.html

5. **Illustrated Explanation of Earned Value**
www.acq.osd.mil/pm/evbasics.htm

6. **NASA Earned Value Management** http://evm.nasa.gov/

EARNED VALUE MANAGEMENT SYSTEM GLOSSARY

ACTUAL COST OF WORK PERFORMED (AC): The cost incurred and recorded in accomplishing the work performed within a given time period.

APPLIED DIRECT COSTS: The amount recognized in the time period associated with the consumption of labor, material, and other direct resources, without regard to the date of commitment or the date of payment. These amounts are to be charged to work–in–progress in the time period that any one of the following occurs:

• When labor, material, and other direct resources are actually consumed.

• When material resources are withdrawn from inventory for use.

• When material resources are received that are identified uniquely to the contract and scheduled for use within 60 days.

• When major components or assemblies are received on a line-flow basis that are identified specifically and uniquely to a single serially numbered end item.

Under this term, material costs may be considered as applied when the articles are received, withdrawn from inventory for use, or applied to the end item.

APPORTIONED EFFORT: Effort that is not readily divisible into work packages, but is related proportionately to measured effort.

AUTHORIZED WORK: Effort that has been definitized and is in the project plan, plus that for which definitized contract costs have not been agreed to, but for which written authorization has been received.

BOTTOM–UP COST ESTIMATE: Estimate derived by summing detailed cost estimates of the individual work packages and adding appropriate burdens. Usually determined by an organization's engineering, price analysis, and cost accounting staffs.

BUDGET AT COMPLETION (BAC): The total budget allocated to any individual PWBS element or defined portion of the contract. The BAC may change due to contract changes, internal replanning, and management reserve applications.

Note: The sum of PWBS element BAC's plus undistributed budget and management reserve should equal the Project Budget Base.

COMMITMENT: An identification of the cost of items on order within an organization's accounting system.

CONTROL ACCOUNT: A management control point at which budgets (resource plans) and actual costs are accumulated and compared to earned value for management control purposes.

A control account is a natural management point for planning and control since it should represent the work assigned to one responsible organizational element on one project work breakdown structure element.

COST ACCOUNTING: A system of accounting analysis and reporting on costs of production of goods or services; or of operation of programs, activities, junctions or organizational units. The system may also embrace cost estimating, determination of cost standards based on engineering data, and comparison of actual and standard costs for the purpose of aiding cost control.

COST PERFORMANCE INDEX (CPI): A measure of cost efficiency comparing the value of work achieved for a dollar of cost.

COST VARIANCE (CV): The difference between work performed (EV) and actual costs (AC) incurred for that specified work.
EV - AC = CV

DIRECT COSTS: The costs or resources expended in the accomplishment of work which are directly charged to the affected project.

DISCRETE EFFORT: Tasks which are related to the completion of specific end products or services and can be directly planned and measured (also may be known as work package effort).

EARNED VALUE (EV): see definition of Value for Work Performed (EV).

ESTIMATE AT COMPLETION (EAC): Actual direct costs, plus indirect costs allocable to the project plus estimate of costs (direct and indirect) for authorized work remaining (may be factored by the CPI).

ESTIMATE TO COMPLETE (ETC): Estimate of costs to complete all work from a point in time to the end of the project (may be factored by the CPI).

GENERAL AND ADMINISTRATIVE (G&A): Those Indirect Costs incurred in the general management of the company, not related to a specific product output (e.g. corporate office, accounting, personnel administration).

INDIRECT COSTS: Costs which, because of their incurrence for common or joint objectives, are not readily subject to treatment as direct costs.

INTERNAL REPLANNING: Replanning actions performed by the company for remaining effort within the recognized total allocated budget.

LEVEL OF EFFORT (LOE): Effort of a general or supportive nature that does not produce specific end products.

MANAGEMENT RESERVE (MR): Management Reserve or Management Reserve Budget. An amount of the total allocated budget withheld for management control purposes, rather than designated for the accomplishment of a specific work package or set of Work Packages. It is not a part of the Performance Measurement Baseline (sometimes called contingency).

MANPOWER SCHEDULING AND LOADING: The effective, efficient utilization and scheduling of available manpower according to their skills to ensure that required operations are properly staffed and executed.

MATERIAL: Property which may be incorporated into or attached to an end item to be delivered under a contract or which may be consumed or expended in the performance of a contract. It includes, but is not limited to, raw and processed material, parts, components, assemblies, fuels and lubricants, and small tools and supplies which may be consumed in normal use in the performance of a project (may include purchased/leased labor).

NETWORK SCHEDULE: A schedule format in which the activities and milestones are represented along with the interdependencies between activities. It expresses the logic of how the project work will be accomplished. Network schedules are the basis for critical path analysis, a method for identification and assessment of schedule priorities and impacts.

OTHER DIRECT COSTS: Usually the remaining direct costs, other than labor and material, like travel and computer costs.

OVERHEAD: (See indirect costs) Those indirect costs which are incurred in support of the direct cost functions producing the company's output. (e.g. engineering management, factory maintenance, tool maintenance, tool room personnel).

PERFORMANCE MEASUREMENT BASELINE (PMB): The time phased budget plan against which project performance is measured. It is formed by the budgets assigned to scheduled control accounts and the applicable indirect budgets. For future effort, not planned to the control account level, the performance measurement baseline also includes budgets assigned to higher level project work breakdown structure elements and undistributed budgets. It equals the total allocated budget, less management reserve.

PERFORMING ORGANIZATION: A defined unit within the company's organizational structure, which applies the resources to perform the work.

PLANNED VALUE FOR WORK SCHEDULED (PV): The sum of planned budgets for all work packages, planning packages, etc., scheduled to be accomplished (including in-process work packages), plus the amount of level-of-effort and apportioned effort scheduled to be accomplished within a given time period.

RESOURCE PLAN: The time-phased budget, which is the schedule for the planned expenditure of project resources for accomplishment of project work scope.

PLANNING PACKAGE: A logical aggregation of work within a control account, normally the far term effort, that can be identified and budgeted in early baseline planning, but is not yet defined into detailed work packages.

REPLANNING: Replanning actions for remaining work scope. A normal project control process accomplished within the scope, schedule, and cost objectives of the program.

RESPONSIBLE ORGANIZATION: A defined unit within the organizational structure that is assigned responsibility for accomplishing specific tasks.

SCHEDULE: A series of events to be done in sequence within a given time period.

SCHEDULE TRACEABILITY: Compatibility between schedule due dates, status and work scope requirements at all levels of schedule detail (vertical traceability) and between schedules at the same level of detail (horizontal traceability).

SCHEDULE PERFORMANCE INDEX (SPI): A measure of schedule efficiency comparing the value of work achieved to the planned value of work scheduled.

SCHEDULE VARIANCE (SV): The difference between EV and PV for a specific work elements. EV - PV = SV.

SCOPE OF WORK (SOW): The document that defines the work scope requirements for a project.

SIGNIFICANT VARIANCES: Those differences between planned and actual performance requiring further reviews, analysis, or action. Thresholds should be established as the magnitude of variances that will require variance analysis, and the thresholds should be revised as needed to provide meaningful analysis during execution of the project.

UNDISTRIBUTED BUDGET (UB): The budget applicable to known and scheduled project effort which has not yet been identified to a specific WBS element for detailed planning at or below the lowest level or reporting to the customer.

VALUE FOR WORK PERFORMED (EV): The sum of the budgets planned for completed work packages and completed portions of open work packages plus the applicable portion of the budgets for level of effort and apportioned effort. This is also known as the Earned Value.

WORK BREAKDOWN STRUCTURE (WBS): Task or product–oriented family tree division of hardware, software and services that organize and define the product and is the basis for correlating schedule, budget, cost and performance measurement.

WORK PACKAGE (WP): A detailed, short time span job or material item identifying work required to complete a project effort. It is a discrete unit of work having clear identification from all other work; a single control account and organizational identity; budget in measurable units; scheduled start and completion; and a definable end result.

Acronyms

AC – Actual Cost

ACWP – Actual Cost of Work Performed (a.k.a. Actual Cost)

AWP – Authorized Work Package (sometimes called Open Work Package)

BAC – Budget at Completion

BCWP – Budgeted Cost of Work Performed (a.k.a. Earned Value)

BCWS – Budgeted Cost of Work Scheduled (a.k.a. Planned Value)

CA – Control Account

CAM – Control Account Manager

CP – Critical Path

CPI – Cost Performance Index

CPM – Critical Path Method

CPR – Cost Performance Report

C/SCSC – Cost/Schedule Control System Criteria (a.k.a. CommonSense Cost and Schedule Comparison

CV – Cost Variance

DE – Discreet Effort

DOD – Department of Defense

EAC – Estimate at Completion

ERP – Enterprise Resource Planning

ETC – Estimate to Completion

EV – Earned Value

EVMS – Earned Value Management Systems (a.k.a. Every Variance Means Something)

FAA – Federal Aviation Administration
G&A – General and Administrative
LOE – Level of Effort
LRE – Latest Revised Estimate
MR – Management Reserve
MRP – Material Resource Planning; Manufacturing Resource Planning
NASA – National Aeronautic and Space Administration
OAC – Other Allocated Costs
OBS – Organization Breakdown Structure
OI – Objective Indicator (milestones)
OJT – On the Job Training
OLE – Object Linking and Embedding
PD – Project Directive
PDM – Precedence Diagram Method (a.k.a. Activity on Node Method)
PERT – Project Evaluation and Review Technique
PI – Performance Indices
PMB – Performance Measurement Baseline
PMBOK – Project Management Body of Knowledge
PMI – Project Management Institute
PMP – Project Management Professional (certification by Project Management Institute
PS&O – Purchase Services and Other
PV – Planned Value of Scheduled Work
PWBS – Project Work Breakdown Structure
PWP – Planned Work Package
R&D – Research and Development
RAM – Responsibility Assignment Matrix
SME – Subject Matter Expert

SMO – Subject Matter Zero
SOW – Scope of Work
SPAR – Schedule Problem Analysis Report
SPI – Schedule Performance Index
SV – Schedule Variance
TCPI – To Complete Performance Index
TRVL – Travel and Subsistence
UB – Undistributed Budget
VAC – Variance at Completion
VAR – Variance Analysis Report
WA – Work Authorization
WBS – Work Breakdown Structure
WP – Work Package
WPCR – Work Package Change Record